ANIMALS
of Australia

Ken Stepnell

First published in 2015 by Reed New Holland Publishers Pty Ltd
Sydney

Level 1, 178 Fox Valley Road, Wahroonga, NSW 2076, Australia

www.newhollandpublishers.com

A record of this book is held at the British Library and the National Library of
Australia.

ISBN 978 1 92151 754 9

Managing Director: Fiona Schultz
Publisher and Project Editor: Simon Papps
Designer: Thomas Casey
Production Director: Arlene Gippert
Printed in China

All images by Ken Stepnell except the following: Dreamstime (front cover,
back cover, pages 1, 11, 119 and 176 above; and Simon Papps: p.176 below.

10 9 8 7 6 5 4 3

Keep up with New Holland Publishers:

 NewHollandPublishers

 @newhollandpublishers

CONTENTS

INTRODUCTION

In Australia we are truly blessed with a huge number of unique mammals, reptiles and amphibians. There is a very wide range of species and more than 80 per cent of the mammals, nearly 90 per cent of reptiles and more than 90 per cent of the amphibians found here are endemic to our country.

Frogs

Australia has a great diversity of frogs, with more than 220 different species, and some people believe that this number could be as high as 240 species. This compares to just over 100 species in North America and barely 50 in the whole of Europe. Many Australian frogs are nocturnal and they range in size from the large Southern Frog to the tiny and highly endangered Corroboree Frog. Unfortunately many species of frogs are declining and more species are threatened with extinction than in any other family of animals in Australia. Records show that about 30 per cent of our frog species are under threat or already extinct.

Reasons for this decline include loss or degradation of habitat. Frogs are very vunerable and act as a gauge to measure the conditions of the environment. Humans would be well advised to heed these warnings and take action to remedy the situation as soon as possible.

Reptiles

The number of reptiles in Australia is vast. It is believed that we have over 850 different species, with that number being revised upwards all the time due to new discoveries and reclassifications.

The two species of crocodiles in northern Australia are undoubtedly among the most spectacular. However, it is the lizards where the greatest diversity occurs, with more than 700 species recorded, ranging from the 130 species of gecko, which can be as small as 5cm in length, to the 30 species of monitor, the largest of which is the Perentie, which can grow to over two metres in length.

The skinks are the largest reptile family in Australia. It includes nearly 400 species, ranging in size from around 5cm to the blue-tongues and Shingleback which can grow to six times that length. The dragon family is well represented and although many species are cryptically patterned to blend in with their habitat, whether it be desert, scrub or rainforest, it includes a number of the most spectacular and unique lizard species such as Frilled Lizard, Boyd's Forest Dragon and Thorny Devil.

Australia has also the reputation for having more venomous snakes than any other country in the world. We also have some of the most deadly of snakes in the world, which contain some of the world's most toxic venom. These include the King Brown Snake, the tiger snakes and the taipans.

Australia has around 15 species of non-venomous pythons, which are known for their large size and for the way that they suffocate their prey using constriction before swallowing it. Australia also has more than 30 known species of blind snakes, while more than 30 species of marine sea snake have been recorded in our waters, mainly off northern Australia, and some of these are highly venomous.

Mammals

Australia has a remarkable mammal fauna comprising nearly 400 species, and its geographical isolation has resulted in many of these being quite unique.

Two of the world's five living monotremes are found in Australia: the Platypus and the Short-beaked Echidna. These differ from all other mammals in their breeding habits as both are egg-layers. The amphibious Platypus has a bill like a duck and venomous spurs on its hind-limbs. It is undoubtedly one of the strangest creatures in the animal world and early naturalists considered it so outlandish that they believed it to be a hoax. Echidnas are similarly strange. The body is covered with spines and it can move its tongue in and out of its tubular snout over 100 times a minute as it feeds on termites or ants.

Australia has the world's largest and most diverse range of marsupials. These mammals have a pouch in which to rear their young. Probably the best-known of these are the macropods, the family that includes kangaroos and wallabies. These are found throughout Australia except in the snow regions, with the Red Kangaroo being the largest species at over two metres in length. Members of this family have strong hind-legs for hopping, while the strong tail helps them to balance as they travel at high speeds.

Larger species have been clocked at speeds of over 70km/h. Smaller members of the family include the various species of pademelons, potoroos, bettongs and rat-kangaroos.

Many species of kangaroo and wallaby have benefitted from the recent activities of humans, and the development of pastures has increased their food supply. Their diets vary according to species and location, with some acquiring food by digging out small pieces of root material, fungi and tubers.

The Dasyuridae family includes the quolls, bandicoots and bilbies together with smaller species which are sometimes referred to as 'marsupial mice'. Many of these are found only in the desert regions of inland Australia.

Probably the best-known of all the Australian marsupials is the Koala, which is arboreal and feeds entirely on a selection of eucalyptus leaves. They spend the greatest part of their lives either feeding on gum leaves or sitting and sleeping in a forked branch of a tree. Wombats are entirely different, being ground-dwellers, feeding on grasses or seeds and sheltering in burrows.

The possums are very diverse family of arboreal marsupials, varying in size from the tiny pygmy-possums which weigh only a few grams to the much larger ringtail and brushtail possums. The gliders are included in this family and they have membranes called 'patagiums' which enable them to glide silently from tree to tree with great ease.

Australia is also home to a good selection of species of native mice and rats, many of which inhabit arid areas and, like most other desert creatures, can survive without much moisture.

Our marine mammals include populations of both fur-seals and sea-lions, both of which are recovering after the early European settlers hunted these animals for both food and fur.

Threats

When Australia was settled, many introduced animals were brought here, and unfortunately many have become feral and are a threat to our wildlife. It is believed the first animal introduced was the Dingo, and fossil evidence suggests that it arrived about 5,000 years ago. Much later the Europeans brought a variety of animals, and possibly the worst of these were the fox and cat, which have decimated populations of many native creatures. Other introduced threats include goats, camels, pigs, Water Buffalos and Cane Toads: it would be hard to know which of these has had the worst effect on the native Australian flora and fauna.

With nearly 70 per cent of Australia's land under cultivation, it means that many of the animals in Australia are under threat from habitat loss. It is not too late begin change, but unfortunately the hard sell has not yet begun.

This species in this book

As much as possible this guide attempts to cover common and widespread species, and it also includes some of the specialities from particular regions, states, territories or habitats.

The Latin name is listed alongside the common name as common names are not always universally applied and there are still some local and regional variations.

Each species account gives at least one photograph for identification and also a concise description of the animal's maximum length and its key identification features. The 'Habitat/ Range' section is also of particular importance for ID, as a creature with a limited distribution is unlikely to occur elsewhere.

I hope that this field guide will in some way help to develop interest in our wonderful heritage of animals and to promote their preservation.

THE ANIMALS

Mains Burrowing Frog *Cyclorana maini*

SIZE/ID: 7cm. Olive-brown to grey-brown, possibly with darker greenish patches on back, pale stripe down centre of back and broad dark stripe through eye. Back smooth or slightly warty.

FOOD/BEHAVIOUR: Feeds on insects and larvae. Adapted to survive in dry areas by absorbing water into body, burrowing into ground, encasing itself in a cocoon, and waiting for next rains.

HABITAT/RANGE: Arid areas of Western Australia, South Australia and Northern Territory.

Southern Brown Tree Frog *Litoria ewingii*

SIZE/ID: 7cm. Dorsal colour ranges from dark brown to pale grey, paler on flanks. Dark stripe from nostril, through eye, to shoulder. Conspicuous yellow and black colour on groin. No webbing between fingers, some between toes.

FOOD/BEHAVIOUR: Feeds on invertebrates such as leeches and insects. Able to withstand very cold conditions and will survive even if frozen.

HABITAT/RANGE: Freshwater ponds, lakes and heathlands in southern Victoria, South Australia, New South Wales, Tasmania and Bass Strait Islands.

White-lipped Tree Frog *Litoria infrafrenata*

SIZE/ID: 13cm. Female larger than male. Dorsal surface of head, limbs and fingers usually bright green, but colour variations do occur, mainly because of location. Lower lip has a conspicuous white line. Webbed toes have large pads which enable them to climb easily.

FOOD/BEHAVIOUR: Insects and arthropods make up most of the diet. Can live up to 20 years.

HABITAT/RANGE: Tropical areas of Queensland and northern New South Wales.

Green Tree Frog *Litoria caerulea*

SIZE/ID: 10cm. Usually green, but base colour can vary according to location. Sometimes has small white spots on back. The eyes are golden and have horizontal irises.

FOOD/BEHAVIOUR: Feeds on insects. Very docile and suited to living near homesteads.

HABITAT/RANGE: Widespread in Queensland and Northern Territory, also in northern areas of Western Australia, South Australia and New South Wales. Prefers the tropical warmth of northern Australia.

Magnificent Tree Frog *Litoria splendida*

SIZE/ID: 10cm. A relatively large tree frog. Most individuals have small white or sulphur spots on their backs.

FOOD/BEHAVIOUR: Often found close to human settlements. Spends much of the day in crevices or caves. Mainly nocturnal, most feeding and courtship activity takes place at night.

HABITAT/RANGE: The Kimberley region of north-west Australia.

Growling Grass Frog *Litoria raniformis*

SIZE/ID: 10cm. Mottled bright green, often with dark brown bumps. Cream on underside, pale stripe runs from side of head and down flanks. Thighs usually green.

FOOD/BEHAVIOUR: Feeds on invertebrates, including worms and insects and their larvae. A very agile climber.

HABITAT/RANGE: Often associated with large swamps and permanent water holes in areas of South Australia, Victoria, New South Wales, Tasmania and Bass Strait Islands.

Whistling Tree Frog *Litoria verreauxii verreauxii*

SIZE/ID: 4cm. Pale brown to reddish brown, often with a very distinct dark patch running down back. On head a dark band starts at nostrils and continues across eye and down shoulder.

FOOD/BEHAVIOUR: Feeds on insects, spiders and crustaceans. Males call from waterside vegetation.

HABITAT/RANGE: In swamps, dams and woodlands in coastal areas of Victoria, New South Wales and Queensland.

Spotted Marsh Frog *Limnodynastes tasmaniensis*

SIZE/ID: 4.5cm. Usually pale grey-green or brown with irregular dark patches. Colours variable and sometimes has pale stripe running down back.

FOOD/BEHAVIOUR: Feeds on insects and crustaceans. This species is one of the first to colonise new dams and water holes.

HABITAT/RANGE: Tasmania, Bass Strait Islands, Victoria, New South Wales and Queensland.

Frogspawn of Striped Marsh Frog
Limnodynastes peronii

SIZE/ID: As many as 70 eggs can be laid in a foamy nest. Tadpoles may take up to 12 months to fully develop. Adults similar to Spotted Marsh Frog but with bold stripes running down back.

HABITAT/RANGE: Coastal areas of Victoria, New South Wales and Queensland.

Freshwater Crocodile *Crocodylus johnstoni*

SIZE/ID: 4m. Distinguished from Saltwater Crocodile by long, narrow snout.

FOOD/BEHAVIOUR: Feeds mainly at night on fish, frogs, birds, turtles, crustaceans and other small animals. Female lays eggs in a hole during August–September; they hatch during the wet season. Female helps the young from the eggs and then gently rolls them between her jaws and takes them to the water. When most of the clutch is in the water, the female then mounts a protective watch over them.

HABITAT/RANGE: Endemic to freshwater habitats of northern Australia. Found in northern areas of Western Australia, Northern Territory and Queensland. Widely distributed in freshwater rivers, lagoons, billabongs and water holes.

Saltwater Crocodile *Crocodylus porosus*

SIZE/ID: 5m. Some individuals have reportedly measured over 7m, but 5m is more typical for a fully grown adult. Snout more broad than in Freshwater Crocodile.

FOOD/BEHAVIOUR: Feeds on a variety of domestic and native animals. Dangerous to humans. Breeding season from October–May, or during the onset of the wet; female lays 40–80 eggs. Often sunbathes on riverbank during day and if disturbed will slip into water with hardly a sound. Often seen swimming with just nose and eyes above water.

HABITAT/RANGE: Most frequently found in saltwater environments, but also in freshwater streams, rivers and water holes. Occurs in northern areas of Queensland, Northern Territory and a small area of Western Australia.

Loggerhead Turtle *Caretta caretta*

SIZE/ID: 100cm. Marine reptile with worldwide distribution. Skin colour ranges from yellow to brown, shell reddish-brown. In adults the tail and claws of the male are thicker.

FOOD/BEHAVIOUR: Omnivorous, feeding off the bottom of the ocean. Comes ashore only to nest. In Australia they nest along the coastline in Queensland and Western Australia, in areas where the water temperature is around 28°C. Female digs a hole in the sand in which to lay the eggs.

HABITAT/RANGE: Found in oceans worldwide, including all around coasts of Australia.

Eastern Long-necked Turtle *Chelodina longicollis*

SIZE/ID: 25cm. Variable in colour, but usually brown. Very long neck usually covered with tubercles. Has slight depression on top of head.

FOOD/BEHAVIOUR: Diet mainly consists of frogs, small fish and a variety of aquatic insects. Often seen perched on logs or tree limbs, usually over water.

HABITAT/RANGE: Found in freshwater habitats over much of Victoria, New South Wales and southern Queensland.

Marbled Gecko *Christinus marmoratus*

SIZE/ID: 7cm. One of the most variable species of gecko in Australia. The scales under the tail do not overlap; these can be dark grey or pink. The pattern under the tail is consistent, but the colour of the blotches can vary from red to orange; these markings can be more obvious on young individuals rather than mature ones.

FOOD/BEHAVIOUR: Feeds on insects such as beetles. Each female lays only two eggs at a time. When larger groups occur it is thought that more than one female has laid. Eggs take up to five months to hatch.

HABITAT/RANGE: Sometimes shelters under loose tree bark but less arboreal than other geckos on the Australian mainland, often using the cracks and ledges in limestone for shelter. Occurs in Victoria and southern areas of Western Australia, South Australia and New South Wales.

Tree Dtella *Gehyra variegata*

SIZE/ID: 5.5cm. Colour variable. Some individuals pale brown with bands of pale dots, while others have brown spots enclosed by dark curved bars.

FOOD/BEHAVIOUR: Feeds at night on insects and smaller lizards, but often seen basking in the sun during the day.

HABITAT/RANGE: Arid regions of Western Australia, South Australia, New South Wales, Queensland and Northern Territory; range extends to coasts in Western Australia.

Lesueur's Velvet Gecko *Oedura lesueurii*

SIZE/ID: 8cm. Mainly grey-brown with irregular dark blotches. Paler markings down vertebral region, often from the nape to tail, have ragged dark borders. Tail moderately long.

FOOD/BEHAVIOUR: Main food insects, which are caught while waiting at their rock ledges. These geckos often become prey for tree snakes.

HABITAT/RANGE: Often seen under rock ledges, sandstone or granite boulders. Only in a small area of New South Wales, although range extends just into the south-east corner of Queensland.

DIPLODACTYLIDAE

Northern Spiny-tailed Gecko *Strophurus ciliaris*

SIZE/ID: 9cm. Colour varies greatly, from pale brown to dark grey-brown, with white dots and blotches of orange. Has tubercles along the back, spines above the eye and two rows of spines that run along the tail.

FOOD/BEHAVIOUR: Feeds mainly on insects at night. Able to exude a sticky substance from the spines on the tail as a defence when attacked by predators.

HABITAT/RANGE: Widespread in mainland Australia, except in Victoria.

Western Shield Spiny-tailed Gecko
Strophurus wellingtonae

SIZE/ID: 11cm. Colour ranges from grey to brownish-grey, with up to eight lateral blotches between neck and tail. Has spines on tail and above eyes, and large tubercles in two parallel lines on back.

FOOD/BEHAVIOUR: Small insects make up about 90 per cent of the diet. Like all geckos has the ability to re-grow a lost tail.

HABITAT/RANGE: Usually shelters under stones or logs. Only found in a small area of Western Australia.

Variable Fat-tailed Gecko
Diplodactylus conspicillatus

SIZE/ID: 6cm. Colour ranges from fawn to dark reddish-brown. Body short and plump, tail appears to be flat. Sometimes has a pale streak running from nostril to eye.

FOOD/BEHAVIOUR: Feeds mainly on termites, ants and other insects. Although often considered nocturnal, they are frequently seen in daylight hours. Often finds shelter and protection in vertical spider holes, using tail to block entrance.

HABITAT/RANGE: Found in all mainland states except Victoria, in the interior and north to the coast of Northern Territory.

Thick-tailed Gecko *Underwoodisaurus milii*

SIZE/ID: 12cm. Pink to dark brown with some yellow spots centred on tubercles. Carrot-shaped tail tapers to a pointed tip.

FOOD/BEHAVIOUR: Feeds at night, mainly on insects, spiders and small arthropods. Like many geckos will lick its eyes after a meal; it is thought that this is in order to keep the eyelids clean.

HABITAT/RANGE: Often found sheltering in heathland, in shrubs or under rock ledges. Occurs in the southern half of Australia, as far north as southern Queensland and Northern Territory, although absent from Tasmania and coastal Victoria.

Smooth Knob-tailed Gecko *Nephrurus levis*

SIZE/ID: 10cm. Pale pink to purplish brown, usually with three darker bands crossing the head, neck and shoulder. Body and limbs covered with small orange and yellow tubercles. Tail usually plump and often heart-shaped.

FOOD/BEHAVIOUR: Feeds on insects such as beetles and flies, other small invertebrates and small geckos.

HABITAT/RANGE: Found in dry inland areas in all mainland states except Victoria.

Gidgee Skink *Egernia stokesii*

SIZE/ID: 15cm. Colour variable; usually reddish-brown with irregular pale blotches. Each dorsal has two spines. Cone-shaped tail covered in spines. Also called Stokes' Skink.

FOOD/BEHAVIOUR: Feeds on small animals, insects such as grasshoppers and crickets, fruit and some plants. Often seen on or near rock ledges. If alarmed can wedge itself into a small crevice, puff out the body, and with spurs extended it is impossible to move them.

HABITAT/RANGE: Western parts of Western Australia and an area covering eastern South Australia, western New South Wales and southern Queensland and Northern Territory.

Cunningham's Skink *Egernia cunninghami*

SIZE/ID: 20cm. Colour varies from black to very dark brown. Tail long with one spine on each dorsal scale.

FOOD/BEHAVIOUR: Feeds on insects such as crickets and other small animals. Like all skinks often seen sitting on rocks or ledges. Will also use logs for shelter.

HABITAT/RANGE: Found in areas of Victoria, New South Wales and a small portion of Queensland.

King's Skink *Egernia kingii*

SIZE/ID: 24cm. Colour ranges from black and dark brown to olive. Most frequently plain, although some individuals have a small number of pale spots.

FOOD/BEHAVIOUR: Feeds on insects and their larvae, as well as eggs from seabird rookeries. Often seen basking on rock ledges and among the coastal heath. Shelters in old burrows of shearwaters and penguins.

HABITAT/RANGE: Occurs only in south-west Western Australia, including on some offshore islands.

Hosmer's Skink *Egernia hosmeri*

SIZE/ID: 18cm. Colour usually light yellow-brown to cream, with some dark blotches. Usually three or four sharp keels on each dorsal, with only one on the cylindrical tail. Body is spiny and nearly half of the tail is covered with long spines.

FOOD/BEHAVIOUR: Feeds on insects, berries and fresh new shoots of plants. When alarmed it wedges between rocks, puffs out its body and the spines grip the rocks, making it almost impossible to displace.

HABITAT/RANGE: In areas of Queensland and Northern Territory. Often found under rocks or in crevices.

Bougainville's Skink *Lerista bougainvillii*

SIZE/ID: 7cm. From silver-grey to light brown, sometimes with red or yellow markings on tail. Some individuals have dark lines across the back and a broad stripe.

FOOD/BEHAVIOUR: Feeds at night mainly on arthropods and insects. Rarely seen in daylight. Spends much of its life under cover.

HABITAT/RANGE: Found in areas of South Australia, Victoria, New South Wales and a small part of Tasmania.

Desert Rainbow-Skink *Carlia triacantha*

SIZE/ID: 5cm. Greyish to brown, with a faint pale stripe under eye. A slender skink with a long tail. Ear opening vertical and elongated. Males have prominent reddish-orange lateral flush with a broad midlateral stripe on chin and speckled pale blue throat.

FOOD/BEHAVIOUR: Feeds on small vertebrates and insects. Well adapted to desert conditions.

HABITAT/RANGE: Mainly the arid areas of Western Australia and Northern Territory, in woodlands, spinifex and sandy country.

Leopard Ctenotus *Ctenotus pantherinus*

SIZE/ID: 11cm. Very robust. Olive to copper-brown, depending on location. Uneven rows of pale-centred dark ocelli on body. In addition some individuals may have off-white spots.

FOOD/BEHAVIOUR: Feeds on a variety of insects, small arthropods and some plant material. One of the most widespread members of its large genus; there are over 100 species of *Ctenotus* skink in Australia.

HABITAT/RANGE: Occurs in all mainland states except Victoria.

Eastern Striped Skink *Ctenotus robustus*

SIZE/ID: 13cm. From brown to olive brown, with a black stripe that is very prominent along the back. The upper flanks are mainly olive brown to dark brown.

FOOD/BEHAVIOUR: Feeds on small animals, arthropods, crickets and snails. Like all skinks they lay eggs; usually two or three small white eggs are laid.

HABITAT/RANGE: Found over all mainland states, from tropical areas to dry woodland and heath areas.

Southern Water Skink *Eulamprus tympanum*

SIZE/ID: 9.5cm. From brown to black on back and sides, with a variety of spots and blotches. Large blotches between the ears and forelimbs, with a pale stripe running back from the ear.

FOOD/BEHAVIOUR: Arthropods, insects and small lizards form the main part of the diet. These skinks are diurnal and very shy. They use rocks, logs and burrows for egg-laying.

HABITAT/RANGE: Eastern New South Wales, southern Victoria and south-east South Australia.

Pink-tongued Skink *Cyclodomorphus gerrardii*

SIZE/ID: 45cm. Mainly slate grey with dark brown or black bands, more pronounced in male than female. Tip of snout is pale in colour, tongue and mouth are blue in immatures, with a pink tongue developing when adult.

FOOD/BEHAVIOUR: Feeds on slugs, snails and some vegetation. When threatened raises body off ground and flicks out tongue, rather like a snake.

HABITAT/RANGE: Eastern New South Wales and Queensland, from Cairns to Sydney. Inhabits wet forest areas and shelters in hollow logs and under rocks.

Western Blue-tongue *Tiliqua occipitalis*

SIZE/ID: 32cm. Colour variable from yellowish-brown to grey-brown. Four to six broad dark bands on body, and a broad dark stripe runs from eye through ear. One of six species of blue-tongue in Australia. When threatened opens mouth and sticks out blue tongue as a threat.

FOOD/BEHAVIOUR: Diurnal, feeding on insects, spiders, snails, carrion and plant-matter. Very slow-moving.

HABITAT/RANGE: Widespread in South Australia and southern Western Australia. Range extends into southern Northern Territory, north-west Victoria and south-west New South Wales. Favours grassland, heathland, mallee dunes, shrubs and spinifex.

Centralian Blue-tongue *Tiliqua multifasciata*

SIZE/ID: 29cm. From pale grey to orange with up to 14 bands of either yellow or light brown rings on body. A very prominent black stripe runs from in front of eye to near ear.

FOOD/BEHAVIOUR: Feeds on insects, arthropods, vegetable matter and some smaller animals. Will use spinifex and similar material for shelter.

HABITAT/RANGE: Occurs mainly in the arid interior of Australia, in all states except Victoria. Range extends to coast in northern Western Australia.

Blotched Blue-tongue *Tiliqua nigrolutea*

SIZE/ID: 30cm. Brown to black with large pale blotches, usually white to yellow, but sometimes salmon-coloured. Colour varies depending on location. Tail long and thick, with a smooth scaly appearance.

FOOD/BEHAVIOUR: Omnivorous, eating whatever they find, including prey such as beetles.

HABITAT/RANGE: Widespread in Victoria and Tasmania, also occurs in south-east South Australia and south-east New South Wales. Prefers cool temperate forest areas.

Shingleback *Tiliqua rugosa*

SIZE/ID: 31cm. Colour variable and can include black, grey and many different shades of brown. Robust with blunt head, stumpy tail and smooth scales on body. This species has a number of colloquial names, including 'sleepy lizard', 'bob-tail' and 'stumpy-tail'.

FOOD/BEHAVIOUR: Omnivorous, feeding on snails, carrion and plants. When disturbed they will give a hissing sound as a warning.

HABITAT/RANGE: In southern Australia north to central Queensland, but absent from Tasmania. Found in a variety of habitats from dry areas to wet forests.

Jacky Lizard *Amphibolurus muricatus*

SIZE/ID: 14cm. Robust dragon with well-developed nuchal and vertebral crest. Thighs covered with a scattering of large spiny scales. Colour and pattern varies according to sex and location; generally grey to light brown, paler in hotter climates, darker in cool areas.

FOOD/BEHAVIOUR: Feeds on small vertebrates and insects such as flies and crickets. Often seen perched on tree limbs.

HABITAT/RANGE: Woodland, forest and heath areas. Widespread in Victoria and eastern New South Wales, range extends into south-east South Australia and south-east Queensland.

Long-nosed Dragon *Amphibolurus longirostris*

SIZE/ID: 16cm. Red-brown, brightest on head. Tail very long, often three times longer than body. Slender with long limbs and snout. Has two prominent pale lines running down sides of back and a black patch behind each ear.

FOOD/BEHAVIOUR: Variable diet includes insects and other small creatures. Often seen lying on tree limbs basking in the sun.

HABITAT/RANGE: Mostly arboreal. Range incorporates arid areas of Northern Territory and South Australia west to central coast of Western Australia.

Gilbert's Dragon *Amphibolurus gilberti*

SIZE/ID: 12cm. Female grey to brown, male more blackish. Has bold pale stripe running from behind each eye to base of tail. Has well-developed crest with a continuous vertebral row of enlarged scales.

FOOD/BEHAVIOUR: Feeds on insects such as crickets. Also known as the 'ta-ta lizard' because often waves a leg, similar to people waving goodbye.

HABITAT/RANGE: Northern areas of Western Australia, Northern Territory and Queensland.

Frilled Lizard *Chlamydosaurus kingii*

SIZE/ID: 50cm. Large frill around neck obvious even when folded; frill extended when disturbed. Usually brown but breeding males have reddish, golden or yellow on the frill.

FOOD/BEHAVIOUR: Feeds mainly on beetles that they catch in trees. In the wet season they can be seen perched a few metres from the ground, in the dry season they are rarely seen, when they run they only use their hind legs.

HABITAT/RANGE: Arboreal. North of Western Australia and Northern Territory and northern and eastern Queensland.

Tawny Dragon *Ctenophorus decresii*

SIZE/ID: 19cm. A flat-bodied rock dragon with a smooth snout. Colour varies from grey to brown, usually more orange-brown on head. A dark stripe along each side of body is underlined with a paler stripe. Smooth keeled scales on nose with pale tubercles over back and no keels on vertebral line.

FOOD/BEHAVIOUR: Feeds on insects and other small animals. Very territorial against other dragons.

HABITAT/RANGE: Only in a small area of eastern South Australia. Usually seen on rocky outcrops, basking in the sun.

Painted Dragon *Ctenophorus pictus*

SIZE/ID: 28cm. Mainly brown to yellowish, with dark-edged or pale bars. Has a stout, rounded, blunt head, short legs and a long tail.

FOOD/BEHAVIOUR: Food mainly arthropods, but ants and other insects make up some of the diet. They dig small burrows to shelter in.

HABITAT/RANGE: Found in semi-arid regions. Widespread in Southern Australia, also occurs in adjacent areas of Western Australia, Northern Territory, Queensland, New South Wales and Victoria.

Central Netted Dragon *Ctenophorus nuchalis*

SIZE/ID: 16cm. Usually pale yellowish-brown with dark blotches, numerous small pale spots and a narrow pale vertebral stripe. Very distinct shape with short and plump body, very blunt head and short limbs. Small spiny nuchal crest and up to 34 femoral and preanal pores which sweep in a curve to the thigh.

FOOD/BEHAVIOUR: Diet mainly ants and other insects. Shelters in burrows at base of shrubs; in winter some of the exits are plugged with dirt.

HABITAT/RANGE: Occurs in all mainland states except Victoria. Widespread in deserts and arid regions away from coasts.

Peninsula Dragon *Ctenophorus fionni*

SIZE/ID: 12cm. A flat-bodied rock dragon with a smooth nose and scales on snout. Colour of male dark brownish and densely speckled with orange to brick red. Female colour varies greatly according to location.

FOOD/BEHAVIOUR: Feeds on a variety of insects. Male can often be seen sitting on rocks performing a variety of head bobs and tail swishes.

HABITAT/RANGE: Shelters in rock crevices. Only in central and southern South Australia, including offshore islands.

Lake Eyre Dragon *Ctenophorus maculosus*

SIZE/ID: Male 11.5cm, female 10cm. One of the smaller dragons. Eyes small and sunken and protected from salt by serrated eyelids. Whitish to pale brown with dark flecking and two rows of dark blotches between neck and hips. Both sexes develop red ventral flush during breeding season.

FOOD/BEHAVIOUR: Insects form 70 per cent of diet. Feeds on ants from ant mounds and insects that get trapped in the salt. They seek shelter among the salt crusts. When Lake Eyre is flooded these dragons burrow under the salt crust.

HABITAT/RANGE: Only in the Lake Eyre area of South Australia.

Central Military Dragon *Ctenophorus isolepis*

SIZE/ID: 12cm. Colourful male is reddish-brown with dark-edged white spots on body. Female mainly brown with no black marks.

FOOD/BEHAVIOUR: Feeds on insects and other small creatures, These dragons appear to spend much of their day on the ground, although they will shelter in spinifex.

HABITAT/RANGE: Mainly found in arid regions in the interior of South Australia, Northern Territory, Western Australia and western Queensland. Range extends to coast in north-west Western Australia.

Lozenge-marked Dragon *Ctenophorus scutulatus*

SIZE/ID: 12cm. Pale reddish to grey-brown, with bars on neck and body. Has long tail and limbs.

FOOD/BEHAVIOUR: Feeds on a variety of small insects and similar food. Can move very swiftly if alarmed.

HABITAT/RANGE: Prefers rocky outcrops and arid areas in western and central Western Australia.

Western Heath Dragon *Rankinia adelaidensis*

SIZE/ID: 6cm. Grey to light brown. Wide vertebral stripe is edged with white or off-white blotches. Dark dorsal lines, plus a row of elaborate upper lateral markings.

FOOD/BEHAVIOUR: Feeds mainly on insects, including ants, as well as other small creatures. Like the majority of dragons, if frightened they will move swiftly.

HABITAT/RANGE: Dry coastal regions of south-west Western Australia.

Southern Angle-headed Dragon
Hypsilurus spinipes

SIZE/ID: 15cm. Varying shades of grey, green and light brown. Some individuals have irregular markings or blotches. A row of spines runs from back of neck to tail.

FOOD/BEHAVIOUR: Feeds on spiders, insects and centipedes. This species is slow-moving compared to other dragons.

HABITAT/RANGE: Coastal areas of New South Wales and Queensland.

Boyd's Forest Dragon *Hypsilurus boydii*

SIZE/ID: 16cm. Colours include purplish-brown, green and grey, while both sides of the neck are flushed with dark grey. Large spines on back of head and neck, rows of smaller spines running down back and down centre of throat.

FOOD/BEHAVIOUR: Feeds on insects such as crickets, spiders and other forest creatures.

HABITAT/RANGE: Known range restricted to a small area of tropical Queensland centred around Cairns. Considering that these dragons only frequent tropical rainforest, they could occur in other areas of the state.

Thorny Devil *Moloch horridus*

SIZE/ID: 16cm. Colour usually rich reddish-brown with patches of grey and white. Covered with large thorn-like spines.

FOOD/BEHAVIOUR: Feeds entirely on ants; it is estimated that an individual will eat about 5,000 ants per day. A sticky substance on the tongue helps them to catch the ants. Walks slowly with a jerky movement; tail usually held upright. Has the ability to absorb water through the body.

HABITAT/RANGE: Widespread in arid areas of Western Australia, South Australia and Northern Territory.

Eastern Water Dragon *Intellagama lesueurii*

SIZE/ID: 40cm. Dark olive-green to grey with row of spines on back of head. Can show dark patch behind eye and dark barring on back and tail. During breeding season males become very colourful with orange or golden colour on chest and throat.

68

FOOD/BEHAVIOUR: Feeds on insects and small animals such as crabs, carrion and plants. Often seen resting on tree limbs or logs above water; when frightened will slip quietly into water where they can remain out of sight for some time.

HABITAT/RANGE: Range extends along east coast from eastern Victoria to north-east Queensland.

Eastern Bearded Dragon *Pogona barbata*

SIZE/ID: 26cm. Usually brown, but there is some colour variation according to location. Has a broad row of long spines across the throat and extending onto flanks. When in danger puffs up body, raises head and exposes bright yellow mouth.

FOOD/BEHAVIOUR: Omnivorous. Often seen sunbathing after rain.

HABITAT/RANGE: Found a variety of habitats in eastern Queensland, eastern New South Wales, Victoria and south-east South Australia.

Dwarf Bearded Dragon *Pogona minor*

SIZE/ID: 16cm. Colour usually dull grey to brown, with only a very small beard. Some individuals may have small spines on back.

FOOD/BEHAVIOUR: Feeds on a large and varied diet of insects. Often seen perched on termite mounds, basking in the sun.

HABITAT/RANGE: Prefers arid woodland regions in Western Australia, western South Australia and south-west Northern Territory.

Central Bearded Dragon *Pogona vitticeps*

SIZE/ID: 27cm. This robust dragon is well named because of the pouch-like projection on the throat. Colour can vary greatly and individuals can be yellow, grey, brown, whitish or orange. Has a row of spines across the throat, one or two rows of spines along the flank and a straight row of spines at rear of head. Inside of mouth is pink.

FOOD/BEHAVIOUR: Feeds mainly on insects, smaller lizards, snails and plants. On cool days can often be seen basking in sun.

HABITAT/RANGE: Prefers arid areas in the interior of eastern Australia. Found in eastern South Australia, eastern Northern Territory, western Queensland, western New South Wales and north-west Victoria.

Nullabor Bearded Dragon *Pogona nullarbor*

SIZE/ID: 15cm. Shades of orange, brown and grey with irregular narrow pale bands on back and tail. Beard is small compared to other bearded dragons, with only short spines. Inside of mouth is orange.

FOOD/BEHAVIOUR: Feeds on snails and vegetation. Often seen basking in sun on tree limbs.

HABITAT/RANGE: Only found in a small area of the Nullarbor in south-east Western Australia and south-west South Australia.

Lined Earless Dragon *Tympanocryptis lineata*

SIZE/ID: 7cm. Colouration variable, from shades of brown to grey or brick red. Often with darker bars or patches. Top of head is scaled, rough and keeled.

FOOD/BEHAVIOUR: Insectivorous; sometimes seen by roadside feeding on road-kill insects.

HABITAT/RANGE: Widespread scattered distribution in arid areas throughout mainland Australia.

Pygmy Mulga Monitor *Varanus gilleni*

SIZE/ID: 38cm. Arboreal monitor. Mainly grey to reddish brown with dark reticulations on head and narrow dark bars down body and tail. Nostrils appear to be positioned at sides of nose.

FOOD/BEHAVIOUR: Feeds on insects, smaller lizards, small animals, birds and eggs. Often shelters under large rocks.

HABITAT/RANGE: Mainly in desert regions of Western Australia, South Australia and Northern Territory.

Pilbara Rock Monitor *Varanus pilbarensis*

SIZE/ID: 47cm. Head, neck and body usually dark reddish. Bands of grey ocelli around body. Tail strongly banded black, white and grey.

FOOD/BEHAVIOUR: Feeds on small animals, insects and carrion. Often shelters in rock crevices.

HABITAT/RANGE: Only found in Pilbara region of Western Australia.

Mitchell's Water Monitor *Varanus mitchelli*

SIZE/ID: 70cm. A very slender monitor with a laterally flattened tail. Dark grey to black with lots of yellow spots. Throat and neck have some dark spots and are flushed with yellow.

FOOD/BEHAVIOUR: Feeds on carrion, frogs, fish and invertebrates. Always associated with trees like those in the genus *Pandanus*.

HABITAT/RANGE: Often around swamps and lagoons; it is not uncommon to see this monitor in water. Found in the northern areas of Western Australia and Northern Territory.

Yellow-spotted Monitor *Varanus panoptes*

SIZE/ID: 1.4m. A very robust monitor with a short thick tail. Colour can be black, blackish-brown or red, with rows of black spots extending almost to end of tail. Also called Yellow-spotted Goanna.

FOOD/BEHAVIOUR: Feeds on fish, mice, insects and many other small animals, both native and introduced species. This monitor is an active hunter which will chase down prey, overpower the creature, then eat it.

HABITAT/RANGE: Found northern parts of Western Australia, Northern Territory and Queensland. It is thought that the toxicity of introduced Cane Toads may have killed up to 90 per cent of the population of these monitors.

Heath Monitor *Varanus rosenbergi*

SIZE/ID: 1.5m. Mainly dark grey with fine yellow and white spotting. It has black bands on the body and down the tail.

FOOD/BEHAVIOUR: Feeds on small reptiles, birds, mammals, eggs and carrion. Female can lay up to 15 eggs and usually digs a burrow in a termite mound in January. The eggs hatch from September, often the adults will help the young from the mound.

HABITAT/RANGE: Scattered populations in areas of southern Western Australia, South Australia, Victoria and New South Wales.

Storr's Monitor *Varanus storri*

SIZE/ID: 40cm. A very robust monitor, with a very thick and spiny tail. Pale to dark brown. Densely marked with ocelli on body and limbs. Often has dark streak through eye to ear.

FOOD/BEHAVIOUR: Feeds on insects and other invertebrates. Like all monitors, always on the offensive and swift in movements. During hot weather will feed late in the afternoon or first thing in the morning.

HABITAT/RANGE: In parts of northern Western Australia, Northern Territory and Queensland.

Spiny-tailed Monitor *Varanus acanthurus*

SIZE/ID: 60cm. Most have a blackish or greyish body with silver to yellow spots. Rear of body and tail banded black and rufous.

FOOD/BEHAVIOUR: Feeds mainly on insects such as cockroaches, lizards and other small animals. Thought to obtain about 60 per cent of their water needs from food. A ground-dwelling monitor. Lays up to 18 eggs in a small burrow; they hatch after 3–5 months.

HABITAT/RANGE: Desert areas of northern Western Australia, Northern Territory and north-west Queensland. Often shelters in rock crevices or under shrubs.

Perentie *Varanus giganteus*

SIZE/ID: 2.5m. The largest lizard in Australia. Usually dark brown to grey, with light to whitish patches at regular intervals along the body which form a mosaic-like pattern. Tail tapers to a point.

FOOD/BEHAVIOUR: Like all monitors feeds on carrion, birds, reptiles and other small animals. When frightened looks to escape by climbing anything vertical, and this sometimes includes people if they are nearby!

HABITAT/RANGE: Occurs mainly in desert areas across the centre of Australia, from western Queensland west to the central coast of Western Australia.

Lace Monitor *Varanus varius*

SIZE/ID: 2.1m. One of the best-known monitors; very powerful with long body and long slender tail. Colour ranges from dark grey to blue-black. Has cream to yellow spots on much of body and tail is often banded with yellow.

FOOD/BEHAVIOUR: Feeds mainly on the ground on birds, reptiles and carrion. Will raid poultry sheds. Strong climber, they will often climb trees to escape from danger.

HABITAT/RANGE: Prefers timbered areas. Widespread in Victoria, New South Wales, eastern Queensland and south-east South Australia.

Mertens' Water Monitor *Varanus mertensi*

SIZE/ID: 1m. Mainly dark grey body with many small yellow or cream spots.

FOOD/BEHAVIOUR: Feeds on fish, frogs, carrion and insects. Often seen resting on logs above water; when disturbed will slip quietly into water.

HABITAT/RANGE: Always found near water in northern areas of Queensland, Northern Territory and Western Australia.

Black-headed Monitor *Varanus tristis*

SIZE/ID: 80cm. Head and neck are black, as well the tail is black. Body dark with pale spots or rings. The scales on the head are sharply outlined from the scales on the eyes.

FOOD/BEHAVIOUR: Feeds on reptiles such as smaller lizards. Master of disguise and tends to be secretive. Arboreal and can also be found under rocky ledges or in caves.

HABITAT/RANGE: Found over most of the mainland except southern coasts and Victoria.

Northern Ridge-tailed Monitor *Varanus primordius*

SIZE/ID: 30cm. Grey to reddish brown with many dark spots or flecks on body. No stripes. Area under throat is slightly darker.

FOOD/BEHAVIOUR: Feeds on insects such as termites and crickets, other small animals and carrion. Spends much of time on rocks and rock ledges. Digs small burrows for shelter and protection.

HABITAT/RANGE: Only found in a small area of north-west Northern Territory.

Blackish Blind Snake *Ramphotyphlops nigrescens*

SIZE/ID: 50cm. Colour can be blackish, grey, brown or pink. Body very cylindrical and rigid. Eyes concealed under scales and it is sometimes hard to know which end is the head.

FOOD/BEHAVIOUR: Feeds mainly on small underground creatures such worms. Spends most of life underground, but sometimes surfaces after heavy rain. Lays up to nine small eggs.

HABITAT/RANGE: Northern Victoria, eastern New South Wales and south-east Queensland.

Children's Python *Antaresia childreni*

SIZE/ID: 1m. Colour varies from tan to reddish or purplish-brown. Pattern of numerous smooth-edged and roughly circular blotches can be very noticeable on young snakes but apparently absent on adults.

FOOD/BEHAVIOUR: Feeds on birds, reptiles and small mammals including bats. Very common within its range. Female lays up to 25 eggs; she coils around them to keep them warm and they hatch over a period of about seven weeks.

HABITAT/RANGE: Northern areas of Western Australia and Northern Territory and north-west Queensland, including some offshore islands.

Stimson's Python *Antaresia stimsoni*

SIZE/ID: 88cm. Usually pale brown to cream and irregularly marked with numerous elongated dark blotches. The pattern is prominent and includes a pale ventrolateral line.

FOOD/BEHAVIOUR: Feeds on frogs, lizards and mammals. A 'wait and catch' predator. Like all snakes, able to go for long periods without food.

HABITAT/RANGE: Dry habitats in the interior of all mainland states except Victoria. Range extends to coast in Western Australia.

Spotted Python *Antaresia maculosa*

SIZE/ID: 105cm. Brown with a very prominent pattern of irregular dark blotches over most of the body. Markings appear to have ragged edges.

FOOD/BEHAVIOUR: Feeds on birds, rodents, bats and some other mammals.

HABITAT/RANGE: Found in a variety of habitats, including rocky areas, caves and eucalypt forests. Range extends over much of eastern Queensland and into north-east New South Wales.

Woma *Aspidites ramsayi*

SIZE/ID: Grows to 2.7m. Base colour pale brown or olive, with numerous irregular dark bands and a cream or pale yellow underside. Has similar markings to Black-headed Python, but lacks the black head. Body and head flat. Eyes small.

FOOD/BEHAVIOUR: Feeds on small mammals, birds and reptiles. Nocturnal, sheltering in a burrow or thick vegetation during the day.

HABITAT/RANGE: Desert areas of New South Wales, Northern Territory, Western Australia and South Australia.

Black-headed Python *Aspidites melanocephalus*

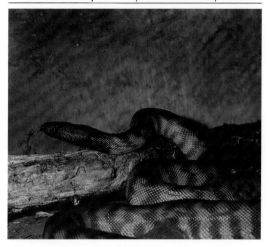

SIZE/ID: 2.5m. Very prominent black head, throat and neck. Body and tail are cream to brown and have numerous dark bands. Colour of the bands varies according to location. Underside can be cream or yellow.

FOOD/BEHAVIOUR: Feeds on frogs, birds and other small animals. Can be either nocturnal or diurnal.

HABITAT/RANGE: Wet tropical areas in the north of Queensland, Northern Territory and Western Australia.

Olive Python *Liasis olivaceus*

SIZE/ID: 4.5m. Australia's second-largest python. Plain dark olive to olive-brown with a pearl-like sheen. Ventral area usually cream. Mid-body scales in 58 rows.

FOOD/BEHAVIOUR: Feeds on birds, mammals including fruit-bats, and reptiles including lizards and even crocodiles. Shelters in and under rock crevices and sometimes in caves.

HABITAT/RANGE: Prefers humid areas; often seen on watercourses and in rocky areas. Occurs in northern areas of Western Australia, Northern Territory and Queensland.

Water Python *Liasis mackloti*

SIZE/ID: 2m, although individuals of 3m have been reported. Uniform dark with iridescence to almost black above. Belly yellow and this includes the first few dorsal scales; also has cream throat.

FOOD/BEHAVIOUR: Feeds mainly on vertebrates. Nocturnal and shelters during the day, often in a hollow log.

HABITAT/RANGE: Found in a variety of habitats, not necessarily near water, in northern areas of Western Australia, Northern Territory and Queensland.

Carpet Python *Morelia spilota*

The most common python in Australia. Head very distinct from body. Can live for up to 30 years. Usually but not always found in wet humid areas. Has been recorded in all mainland states. Non-venomous and kills by constriction; feeds on small animals including rats and mice. Several distinct subspecies occur and four are shown here.

Diamond Python *Morelia spilota spilota*

SIZE/ID: Up to 4m, but most grow to 2m. Many colour variations occur, including gold, yellow or pale brown. Can have black spots or a series of large yellow spots ringed with black.

FOOD/BEHAVIOUR: Nocturnal. Both terrestrial and arboreal. Will often infiltrate flying-fox camps and prey on the animals while they roost.

HABITAT/RANGE: Frequently seen in and around homes or buildings in many areas of Australia from Queensland and New South Wales into Victoria.

Centralian Carpet Python *Morelia spilota bredli*

SIZE/ID: 2m. Mainly brown to reddish-brown with dark-bordered pale markings mainly around the tail. Underside pale cream.

FOOD/BEHAVIOUR: Feeds on lizards and small mammals such as rodents.

HABITAT/RANGE: Restricted to central Australia. Found in dry rocky outcrops in the deserts and mountain regions in the south of Northern Territory.

Jungle Carpet Python *Morelia spilota cheynei*

SIZE/ID: 2.5m. Mainly dark brown, with cream or golden-yellow bands and diamond-shaped blotches, some with a dark centre.

FOOD/BEHAVIOUR: Feeds on small rodents, rabbits and flying-foxes, which they have been known to capture while they hang upside-down.

HABITAT/RANGE: Found in rainforest areas from northern Queensland to northern New South Wales.

Top End Carpet Python *Morelia spilota variegata*

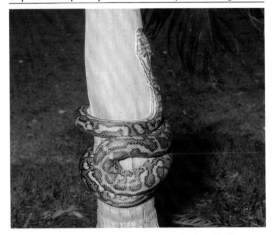

SIZE/ID: 2m. Variable, often with brown ground-colour. Markings can include splashes of blackish-grey and buff cross-bands or stripes.

FOOD/BEHAVIOUR: Feeds on small birds and mammals such as possums.

HABITAT/RANGE: Humid and moist areas in the north of Western Australia and Northern Territory.

Australian Scrub Python *Morelia kinghorni*

SIZE/ID: 4m. The longest snake in Australia. Has a very slender body with broad irregular dark bands and streaks and a milky sheen. Common.

FOOD/BEHAVIOUR: Feeds on birds, fruit-bats, rats, possums and other small animals. Some reports have been made of these snakes taking a small kangaroo or wallaby while they were drinking.

HABITAT/RANGE: Mostly found in the tropical regions of northern Queensland, especially in rainforest areas that are hot and humid with some water.

Desert Death Adder *Acanthophis pyrrhus*

SIZE/ID: 70cm. Various shades of red to brown in colour, with narrow bands of cream or yellow. Body colour often matches habitat.

FOOD/BEHAVIOUR: Highly venomous. Feeds on birds or small animals that come too close. Relies on natural camouflage and deceptively fast strike.

HABITAT/RANGE: Arid areas of Western Australia, northern South Australia, southern Northern Territory and the south-west corner of Queensland.

Northern Death Adder *Acanthophis praelongus*

SIZE/ID: 60cm, female larger than male. Colour ranges from grey to dark brown or reddish-brown. Robust with a strong wrinkled head, strongly keeled dorsal scales with 23 mid-body rows. Tip of tail cream or black.

FOOD/BEHAVIOUR: Highly venomous. Feeds on small animals and insects such as crickets. Like all death adders this species attracts food by flicking tail.

HABITAT/RANGE: Deserts, grasslands and rocky places in northern areas of Western Australia, Northern Territory and Queensland, including offshore islands. Often found among spinifex and other vegetation.

Common Death Adder *Acanthophis antarcticus*

SIZE/ID: 70cm. Moderately robust with a strong head shield and body scales. Colour varies from red-brown to grey, with irregular pale bands between nape and tail. A very dangerous snake; the fangs are long and capable of administering a large amount of venom to a human.

FOOD/BEHAVIOUR: Small lizards and birds. Prefers woodlands and low scrub with plenty of ground litter. When threatened will flatten entire body.

HABITAT/RANGE: Found in a variety of habitats including scrubland, heathland and rocky places. Widespread in Queensland and New South Wales, also occurs in southern Western Australia, southern South Australia, northern Victoria and north-east Northern Territory.

Lowlands Copperhead *Austrelaps superbus*

SIZE/ID: 1.5m. Colour can vary considerably and includes copper, brown, yellow, red or black. Copper head colouring not always present. Some individuals have a dark streak through eye and some have dark bands across nape.

FOOD/BEHAVIOUR: Feeds on lizards, mammals and even members of its own species. A very venomous snake which is capable of killing a human if provoked.

HABITAT/RANGE: Found over much of south-eastern Australia, including Tasmania.

Stephens' Banded Snake *Hoplocephalus stephensii*

SIZE/ID: 1.1m. Colour variable but usually dark grey with narrow brown to cream bands. Some individuals lack banding. Side of head can be blotched or barred with black and white.

FOOD/BEHAVIOUR: Feeds on birds, small lizards, mammals and frogs. Arboreal. During the day often found under loose bark or in tree hollows. Not regarded as dangerous.

HABITAT/RANGE: Restricted to a small area of south-east Queensland and north-east New South Wales.

Southern Tiger Snake *Notechis ater*

SIZE/ID: 1.5m. Can be grey to black in colour, with or without yellowish banding. Many authorities divided it into several subspecies according to location.

FOOD/BEHAVIOUR: Feeds on shearwaters in their nest burrows when in season. Also rats, mice and other small animals. Not aggressive by nature, but the bite is lethal to humans.

HABITAT/RANGE: Western Australia, South Australia, Tasmania, Bass Strait Islands and Kangaroo Island.

Eastern Tiger Snake *Notechis scutatus*

SIZE/ID: 2m. Variable brown to olive, usually with pale bands of various width. Frontal shield is about as long as it is wide and head is relatively flat. Eye fairly large with dark iris and pale-edged pupil. Scales smooth.

FOOD/BEHAVIOUR: Feeds on small animals including birds, frogs and invertebrates. Often found near water. One of the most deadly snakes in Australia.

HABITAT/RANGE: Widespread in Victoria and New South Wales, also in south-east South Australia and south-east Queensland.

Coastal Taipan *Oxyuranus scutellatus*

SIZE/ID: 2m. Reddish-brown to yellowish-brown, some individuals almost black. Head usually paler than body. From 21–23 rows of scales on mid-body.

FOOD/BEHAVIOUR: Feeds on mammals, including rats and even bandicoots. Shelters in old burrows and under logs.

HABITAT/RANGE: Frequents grassy slopes in open country in coastal areas of northern Western Australia, Northern Territory, Queensland and just into New South Wales.

Inland Taipan *Oxyuranus microlepidotus*

SIZE/ID: 2m. Pale yellowish-brown to rich brown in colour. Head and neck glossy black, paler in summer; individuals can change colour according to season.

FOOD/BEHAVIOUR: Feeds almost entirely on rats, and when they are plentiful these snakes breed well. Venom is very toxic to humans, but they are shy and usually retreat rather than attack.

HABITAT/RANGE: A relatively restricted range in inland Queensland, South Australia and New South Wales.

Collett's Snake *Pseudechis colletti*

SIZE/ID: 1.8m. Variable. Can be grey, brown or dark red with some irregular cream or red bands around body.

FOOD/BEHAVIOUR: Feeds on small animals such as rats, birds and frogs. When prey is hard to find can turn to cannibalism. Diurnal, but very secretive in their behaviour and not easy to locate.

HABITAT/RANGE: Only found in a small area of central Queensland.

King Brown Snake *Pseudechis australis*

SIZE/ID: 2.5m. Colour ranges from pale brown to dark blackish, but copper is most common. Dark edges to each scale form reticulated pattern. Ventral surface cream to white. Also called Mulga Snake.

FOOD/BEHAVIOUR: Feeds on a variety of animals including lizards, birds, mammals and frogs. Up to 20 eggs are laid, usually in a small burrow or under a log; they take up two months to hatch and the young are left to fend for themselves.

HABITAT/RANGE: Can occur in any habitat from open arid areas to dense forest, but usually in woodland or scrubland. Absent from rainforest. Widespread and found in all states except Victoria and Tasmania.

Red-bellied Black Snake *Pseudechis porphyriacus*

SIZE/ID: 1.8m. A very glossy black snake with a cream-buff stomach and red pigments extending well up flanks. Like many snakes they are front-fanged.

FOOD/BEHAVIOUR: Diurnal. Feeds mainly on frogs, reptiles and mammals. It is thought that the toxic Cane Toad could have reduced the population of this species. Venomous but rarely deadly to humans.

HABITAT/RANGE: Widespread in Victoria and New South Wales, also occurs in eastern Queensland and south-east South Australia.

Spotted Black Snake *Pseudechis guttatus*

SIZE/ID: 1.5m. A dark-bellied snake, with some midbody scales. Mainly black, sometimes with shades of grey, bluish, pale brown or reddish-brown. Some individuals are creamy with black-tipped scales. Also known as Blue-bellied Black Snake.

FOOD/BEHAVIOUR: Nocturnal. Feeds on small animals such as frogs and reptiles. Shelters in a burrow, log or rock ledge. Has been known to lay up to 16 eggs. Classed as very dangerous to humans.

HABITAT/RANGE: Flood plains, including woodlands which are regularly flooded. Occurs only in a small area of south-east Queensland and north-east New South Wales.

Speckled Brown Snake *Pseudonaja guttata*

SIZE/ID: 1.5m. Orange, brown or yellow with irregular dark bands. Interior of mouth is bluish.

FOOD/BEHAVIOUR: Venomous. Feeds on rats, mice and other small mammals. If provoked will raise body and flatten neck to form a hood. Shelters in open cracks of clay pans.

HABITAT/RANGE: Prefers open grassed areas or open plains country in inland areas of Northern Territory and Queensland.

Curl Snake *Suta suta*

SIZE/ID: 60cm. Olive-brown to dark reddish-brown. Head darker with pale stripe on side. Small pupil is a distinctive feature. Scales dark edged; has 21 midbody scales.

FOOD/BEHAVIOUR: Feeds mostly on small reptiles, mammals and frogs. Name derived from defensive posture when threatened; curls up tightly to protect head and thrashes about. Forages in leaf litter or under rocks, shelters in old burrows or rock crevices. Also called Myall Snake.

HABITAT/RANGE: Widespread in inland areas of Queensland, Northern Territory, South Australia, New South Wales and Victoria. Common in grassland and open bushland.

Platypus *Ornithorhynchus anatinus*

SIZE/ID: 60cm. The most unique mammal in Australia. General description not really necessary because it is so different: a mammal with a bill like a duck and webbed hind-feet. Thick soft fur is brown above, creamy-grey underneath. Tail broad and almost flat.

FOOD/BEHAVIOUR: Invertebrates thought to make up bulk of diet. These are collected from the bottom of a creek and sifted through bill. Constructs burrow just above water-line, sometimes 20m-long. Female usually lays two eggs.

HABITAT/RANGE: Range includes coast of South Australia, Victoria, New South Wales, Queensland and Tasmania. Found in a variety of habitats ranging from rainforest to alpine areas.

Short-beaked Echidna *Tachyglossus aculeatus*

SIZE/ID: 45cm. Dorsal surface of body covered with prickly spines; any fur is between spines. Female lays eggs and suckles young; she has no teats but exudes milk through pores.

FOOD/BEHAVIOUR: Diet includes ants and termites. Highly specialised feeder. Snout and tongue has sticky saliva which is forced into nest chamber and anything that touches it is drawn into mouth. If disturbed can curl into spiny ball or quickly bury itself in soil. In hot climates will shelter under rock ledges, becoming active at night.

HABITAT/RANGE: Widespread across Australia including Tasmania and Bass Strait Islands.

Kowari *Dasyuroides byrnei*

SIZE/ID: 16.5cm. Easily identified by long black brush at tip of tail.

FOOD/BEHAVIOUR: Feeds on insects, small vertebrates and carrion. Obtains all its water from food. Very active at digging, either constructing a burrow or renovating one used by other mammals. Makes a grating call and vigorously twitches tail when threatened.

HABITAT/RANGE: Found only in a small and sparsely vegetated inland area of South Australia and Queensland.

Western Quoll *Dasyurus geoffroii*

SIZE/ID: 35cm. Brown coat with bold white spots and long tail. Differs from Eastern Quoll in range and in having five toes on hind-foot.

FOOD/BEHAVIOUR: Feeds on birds, small animals and carrion. Also raids poultry pens. Has a very explosive call when excited or aggressive. Fast mover on the ground and an excellent climber.

HABITAT/RANGE: Only found in south-west Western Australia – formerly more widespread across the country.

Eastern Quoll *Dasyurus viverrinus*

SIZE/ID: 38cm. A very striking animal with white spots on brown-black fur and very graceful movements. Has large ears, a moist nose and only four toes on hind-foot. Smaller than Spotted-tailed Quoll and lacks spots on tail.

FOOD/BEHAVIOUR: Solitary and opportunistic feeder. Diet includes insects, grubs and birds. Prey such as bandicoots and possums are taken when available. Some grasses and fruits are also part of the diet. Almost entirely a ground-dweller. Shelters in hollow logs or caves.

HABITAT/RANGE: Eucalypt forests, scrub, heathland and some cultivated areas. Only found in Tasmania; formerly more widespread in the south-east of mainland Australia.

Spotted-tailed Quoll *Dasyurus maculatus*

SIZE/ID: 75cm. By far the largest member of this marsupial family and therefore easy to distinguish from other quolls. Rich brown coat with white spots of varying size, including on tail.

FOOD/BEHAVIOUR: Feeds on a variety of birds, reptiles, small mammals including rats, possums and macropods, and other creatures. Excellent climber. Nest can be in a hollow log, tree or rock crevice.

HABITAT/RANGE: Areas of Tasmania, Victoria, New South Wales and Queensland. Spends much of day in forest areas. Mainly nocturnal but will feed and forage in daylight.

Tasmanian Devil *Sarcophilus harrisii*

SIZE/ID: 70cm. Black with white bar across chest and sometimes white spots on rump and back. Short legs, short muzzle, small eyes and broad round ears.

FOOD/BEHAVIOUR: Feeds on almost anything, including frogs, skinks, snakes, bandicoots, sheep, carrion and berries. A nocturnal marsupial with strong jaws. More of a scavenger than a stalker; it is not uncommon for more than one devil to feed on the same carcass. Usually spends the day in a hollow log or other shelter.

HABITAT/RANGE: Tasmania. Prefers forest areas, particularly in the highlands.

Fat-tailed Pseudantechinus
Pseudantechinus macdonnellensis

SIZE/ID: 10.5cm. Grey-brown back, grey-white underparts and chestnut patches behind ears. Tail carrot-shaped, muzzle sharply pointed and eyes bulging.

FOOD/BEHAVIOUR: Diet mainly insects. When food is plentiful the short tail becomes very fat. When food is scarce body can enter torpor and fat stored in tail area is used for energy. Obtains enough water from food to sustain itself. Partly nocturnal; some emerge from burrow or shelter to sunbathe on colder days.

HABITAT/RANGE: Inland desert areas of Western Australia, Northern Territory and South Australia. Mainly found in the rocky hills and termite country.

Yellow-footed Antechinus *Antechinus flavipes*

SIZE/ID: 12cm. A very colourful marsupial with a dark grey head, orange-brown flanks, rufous rump area and blackish-brown tail.

FOOD/BEHAVIOUR: Feeds on plants, nectar, insects, small birds and mice. Farmers are familar with their habits of eating small birds or other vertebrates – the body is turned inside out and the contents devoured. Breeds only once a year.

HABITAT/RANGE: Habitat ranges from tropical forest to open forest and there are even some reports from city areas. Occurs in Victoria, New South Wales, eastern Queensland, south-east South Australia and south-west Western Australia.

Brown Antechinus *Antechinus stuartii*

SIZE/ID: 10cm. Upperparts grey-brown and paler underneath. Head appears to be flat, coming to a point at nose. Tail thin and nearly as long as body.

FOOD/BEHAVIOUR: Feeds mainly at night, sometimes during daylight. Beetles, spiders, cockroaches and arthropods make up most of diet. During two weeks of aggressive courting in August or September, the male spends about six hours a day looking for females and mating; the stress of this kills the male.

HABITAT/RANGE: Occurs in good numbers within its range, particularly in the forest and high rainfall belt in areas of southern Victoria, eastern New South Wales and eastern Queensland.

Brush-tailed Phascogale *Phascogale tapoatafa*

SIZE/ID: 38cm. Mainly grey with cream on stomach and a very bushy black tail which makes ID straightforward; the hairs on the tail can be over 5cm long. Claws are sharp and long for climbing.

FOOD/BEHAVIOUR: Feeds mainly on arthropods, centipedes and small vertebrates. One unusual feature is that the hind-foot can be rotated backwards, enabling the phascogale to climb forwards or backwards with equal ease.

HABITAT/RANGE: Occurs in all mainland states, mainly in the coastal regions.

Fat-tailed Dunnart *Sminthopsis crassicaudata*

SIZE/ID: 8cm. Easy to identify because of the larger ears and by the swollen tail, which is shorter than that of the Stripe-faced Dunnart (*S. macroura*).

FOOD/BEHAVIOUR: Nocturnal, foraging for a variety of foods including invertebrates and small mammals.

HABITAT/RANGE: Widespread in both arid and forest regions in the southern half of Australia, but not along the east coast or in Tasmania. Inhabits a range of low tussocks, grasslands, shrubs, saltbush, gibber country and both desert and open country.

Numbat *Myrmecobius fasciatus*

SIZE/ID: 65cm. One of the most distinctively marked creatures in Australia. The reddish brown and white bands extend from the mid-body to the base of the bushy tail.

FOOD/BEHAVIOUR: Ants and termites are the main food; they are caught by flicking out the sticky tongue. One unusual feature is that it is probably entirely diurnal.

HABITAT/RANGE: Because of their diet they are restricted to a small pocket of wandoo forest in south-west Western Australia.

Northern Brown Bandicoot *Isoodon macrourus*

SIZE/ID: 40cm. Speckled black-brown with a whitish belly; similar in appearance to Southern Brown Bandicoot. Male larger than female, has canine teeth and is more aggressive.

FOOD/BEHAVIOUR: Feeds on invertebrates including insects, spiders and worms. Most food is found above ground, but will occasionally dig with snout. Sleeps for much of day in a small hollow with two entrances. Nest often in a tussock.

HABITAT/RANGE: Prefers wooded areas or other places with plenty of vegetation in northern Western Australia, Northern Territory, Queensland and north-east New South Wales. Like many native animals population has been affected by habitat loss.

Southern Brown Bandicoot *Isoodon obesulus*

SIZE/ID: 34cm Grey-brown to yellow-brown with creamy-white belly. Upper areas of feet and tail are darker brown and ears partly rounded.

FOOD/BEHAVIOUR: Nocturnal. Feeds on insects, larvae, worms and new grass shoots. Prefers to stay close to cover. Sleeps in day in small well-built nests, often made of grass and leaves. Survival of young bandicoots will depend on them finding a suitable area to establish a colony, but once this happens they will quickly go on to breed.

HABITAT/RANGE: Scattered populations found in all states, but biggest concentrations occur along southern coasts of mainland and in Tasmania. Favours rough scrubby areas, especially where burnt.

Eastern Barred Bandicoot *Perameles gunnii*

SIZE/ID: 40cm, male larger than female. Yellow-brown with three or four broad pale bands on sides. Fur takes on a grizzled appearance. Tail almost white.

FOOD/BEHAVIOUR: Feeds on grasses and also digs for worms, insects and larvae. Shelters in a small nest during day.

HABITAT/RANGE: Grassland areas and improved pasture in small area of western Victoria, parts of Tasmania and Bass Strait Islands.

Bilby *Macrotis lagotis*

SIZE/ID: 55cm, male slightly larger than female. Pale grey, hair soft and silky to touch. Nose very pointed and long, ears rabbit-like. Tail black and white with prominent crest; extreme tip of tail is naked.

FOOD/BEHAVIOUR: Feeds on insects, larvae, native fruits, bulbs and fungi. Can go without water for long periods as obtains enough moisture from food. A powerful digger, can burrow up to 3m; entrance often close to termite mound or spinifex for concealment.

HABITAT/RANGE: Favours savannah woodlands, grasslands, tussocks, acacia scrub and spinifex areas. Now only found in the arid regions of Western Australia, Northern Territory and small areas of New South Wales and Queensland.

Koala *Phascolarctos cinereus*

SIZE/ID: 80cm, male slightly larger than female. Mainly grey, sometimes with white chest and inside of ear. One of the few mammals with no tail. Usually solitary. Suited to arboreal life, with claws for climbing and gripping and long arms for reaching food.

FOOD/BEHAVIOUR: Eucalypt leaves are main food, and because these have a high water content drinking is not so necessary. Koalas spend most of their life in trees eating and sleeping, only coming to the ground to find another tree.

HABITAT/RANGE: Found in forest areas of Victoria, New South Wales, Queensland and a small area of South Australia. Occurs in places with suitable eucalypt trees, including river red gum, manna gum and blue gum.

Southern Hairy-nosed Wombat
Lasiorhinus latifrons

SIZE/ID: 93.5cm. Easy to distinguish from Common Wombat due to very hairy snout, much bigger ears and hair which is very silky in appearance.

FOOD/BEHAVIOUR: Feeds on native grasses and low shrubs and rarely has access to water. Well adapted to life in arid regions and able to lower metabolic rate when food is scarce. Appears to be slow, but when in danger can run at speeds of up to 40km/h. Constructs a very extensive warren that can be home to both male and female.

HABITAT/RANGE: Now found only in arid areas in south of South Australia and Western Australia.

Common Wombat *Vombatus ursinus*

SIZE/ID: 98.5cm. Coarse thick hair and large naked nose. Ears short and partly rounded. A very powerful animal, with powerful forelimbs and impressive claws which enable them to dig extensive burrows in a variety of soils; burrows can vary from 2–6m in length.

FOOD/BEHAVIOUR: Herbivorous and feeds mainly on native grasses. Does not require much water, as this is obtained from their food. Mostly nocturnal in summer, but during winter can be seen sunbathing.

HABITAT/RANGE: Found in New South Wales, Victoria, Tasmania and south-east South Australia. Favours bushland and forested areas that are suitable for burrowing. Also occurs in mountain regions.

Mountain Pygmy-Possum *Burramys parvus*

SIZE/ID: 13cm. Mainly grey-brown, paler underneath. Has fine fur and long, thin tail.

FOOD/BEHAVIOUR: Feeds on arthropods, fruits and seeds. Highly terrestrial and very active. The only Australian mammal that is restricted to alpine environments. During winter body has the ability to enter torpor.

HABITAT/RANGE: Restricted to highlands in a small area of eastern Victoria and southern New South Wales.

Eastern Pygmy-Possum *Cercartetus nanus*

SIZE/ID: 10cm. Mainly fawn-coloured with white underparts.

FOOD/BEHAVIOUR: Feeds on insects, pollen and nectar gathered using brush-tipped tongue from native trees including eucalypts, banksias, grevilleas and bottlebrushes. When nectar not available will eat fruit. Mainly nocturnal, usually emerging a few hours after dark. Activity reduced during winter when much of the time is spent in torpor.

HABITAT/RANGE: Found in both wet and dry forests in Tasmania and coastal areas of New South Wales and Victoria. Range extends to south-east Queensland and south-east South Australia.

Leadbeater's Possum *Gymnobelideus leadbeateri*

SIZE/ID: 16cm. Grey to grey-brown body with prominent dark dorsal stripe and much paler chest. They have appealing large eyes which give them great night vision.

FOOD/BEHAVIOUR: Nocturnal feeder on gum, honeydew, spiders and insects such as beetles and tree crickets, most of which live under the bark of eucalypt trees.

HABITAT/RANGE: Only in a very small area of central Victoria. Almost extinct. A colony will nest together in a suitable mountain ash tree, often over 30m high.

Yellow-bellied Glider *Petaurus australis*

SIZE/ID: 28cm. Grey on back, orange-white on chest, black stripe on thigh. Head and body larger than both Sugar and Squirrel Gliders.

FOOD/BEHAVIOUR: Feeds mainly on nectar, pollen, blossom, insects such as cicadas and sap from various trees which is obtained by biting out a small hole. Each glider establishes a territory which incorporates about 20 eucalypt trees. They are very active, running along the underside of branches. Some grooming can take place while the animals hang on with only their hind-feet.

HABITAT/RANGE: Coastal regions of Queensland, New South Wales and Victoria. Prefers tall eucalypt forest in areas with cooler temperatures and high rainfall.

Sugar Glider *Petaurus breviceps*

SIZE/ID: 17cm. Grey body with a black stripe extending from nose across top of head and down back. Tail darker grey. Using membrane between legs it is possible for them to glide distances of 30m.

FOOD/BEHAVIOUR: Nocturnal. Food includes nectar, blossom, pollen and honeydew. In breeding season protein is added to diet by taking spiders and small insects such as beetles and moths. Tail is used to carry material such as fresh leaves and bark for nesting. As many as six gliders have been found using the same nest.

HABITAT/RANGE: Present in all states including Tasmania, in areas where eucalypt forest is prevalent.

Squirrel Glider *Petaurus norfolcensis*

SIZE/ID: 52cm. More than twice as big as Sugar Glider. Grey with white underparts and toes, pale pink nose and dark stripe running from nose over top of head and down back.

FOOD/BEHAVIOUR: Feeds on invertebrates and sap from eucalypt and acacia trees. Like many other native animals is under threat from loss of habitat.

HABITAT/RANGE: Dry sclerophyll forest areas of Victoria, New South Wales and Queensland.

Common Brushtail Possum *Trichosurus vulpecula*

SIZE/ID: 57cm. Easy to identify with very thick silver-grey fur and long and pointed ears and face. Tasmanian race *fuliginosus* is larger. In the past these possums were hunted for their pelts.

FOOD/BEHAVIOUR: Eats most types of fruit, berries and house scraps. Can be a problem for homeowners and gardeners when fruit is ripe. Builds a nest of grass and native plants either in the bush or under

roof of a building. Not uncommon for female to stay in same area for a number of years. Very agile climber which can jump great distances from tree to tree when disturbed.

HABITAT/RANGE: Occurs over much of Australia, including Tasmania. Probably the most common marsupial in Australia.

Common Ringtail Possum *Pseudocheirus peregrinus*

SIZE/ID: 70cm. Large grey-brown possum. Long prehensile tail often used as a fifth limb when climbing or moving from place to place in search of food.

FOOD/BEHAVIOUR: Nocturnal. Feeds on fruit and vegetables. Often lives in close proximity to homes; in many areas considered to be a pest.

HABITAT/RANGE: Widespread in Tasmania, Victoria and New South Wales, also in south-west Western Australia, south-east South Australia and eastern Queensland. Range rarely extends further than a few hundred kilometres from coast.

Rufous Bettong *Aepyprymnus rufescens*

SIZE/ID: 38.5cm, female larger. Distinguished from other macropods by reddish-brown fur and very hairy nose.

FOOD/BEHAVIOUR: Nocturnal feeder on herbs and grasses; forages with strong front claws for roots and tubers of various plants. Like all potoroos, they sleep during the day and if frightened stamp their hind-feet like rabbits.

HABITAT/RANGE: Only found along the east coast of Australia, in Queensland and New South Wales, although there have also been reports from South Australia.

Tasmanian Bettong *Bettongia gaimardi*

SIZE/ID: 60cm. Brownish-grey with white belly. Tail well furred and often has white tip.

FOOD/BEHAVIOUR: Feeds on fungi, seeds, roots and bulbs. Insects have been found in the stomach, but it is thought that these were ingested with the grasses.

HABITAT/RANGE: Now only found in eastern Tasmania, where the open grassy plains suit them well. Also found in eucalypt forests and bushlands.

Woylie *Bettongia penicillata*

SIZE/ID: 33cm. Yellowish-grey with paler underparts. When flushed bounds with head held low and tail almost straight. Has black crest on tail. Also known as Brush-tailed Bettong.

FOOD/BEHAVIOUR: Usually a nocturnal feeder. Underground fungi, bulbs, tubers, insects, grasses and resin seem to make up much of the diet. Water consumption is low. Nest usually domed and often built over a shallow depression and under shrubs or other suitable cover. Tail is used to carry nest material.

HABITAT/RANGE: Formerly widespread but now highly endangered and only found in a few locations in Western Australia. Habitat open forests and woodlands with clumps of tussock and shrubs for cover and shelter.

Northern Bettong *Bettongia tropica*

SIZE/ID: 70cm. Reddish-brown with paler underparts. Little is known about this species, other than the fact that its small area of habitat is under threat from humans.

FOOD/BEHAVIOUR: Like all bettongs feeds at night. Diet includes fruit, seeds, roots and some resin. Daytime is spent in an impressive dome-shaped nest which is built from shredded bark or leaves.

HABITAT/RANGE: Grassy eucalypt forest in a small area of Queensland near Townsville.

Long-footed Potoroo *Potorous longipes*

SIZE/ID: 40cm. Grey to brown on back and much paler underneath. Similar to the more widespread Long-nosed Potoroo (*P. tridactylus*), but with longer hind-feet.

FOOD/BEHAVIOUR: Underground fungi make up the bulk of the diet, but will also take plants and fruit. Terrestrial and obtains much of its food by digging with hind-feet.

HABITAT/RANGE: Found only in a small area of eastern Victoria, in Croajingolong National Park. Favours open forest areas of eucalypt and shrubs, with dense cover of wiregrass, ferns and sedges. These areas usually have high rainfall.

Rufous Hare-Wallaby *Lagorchestes hirsutus*

SIZE/ID: 63cm, female slightly smaller than male. Once common throughout dry areas of Australia and early settlers referred to them as 'spinifex rats'. Even as late as the 1930s it was still prevalent in sandy inland regions.

FOOD/BEHAVIOUR: Diet restricted to plants containing high fibre, young leaves, seeds of desert plants and new shoots of spinifex. Feeds at night and shelters from heat of day under desert vegetation.

HABITAT/RANGE: Today only found in inland desert regions of Northern Australia, South Australia and parts of Western Australia. It is believed that traditional Aboriginal burning methods favoured this species by resulting in suitable ground cover of stunted desert foliage.

Agile Wallaby *Macropus agilis*

SIZE/ID: 80cm, male larger than female. Sandy-brown with off-white chest. Tip of tail and tips of ears are black. Has pale band under eye.

FOOD/BEHAVIOUR: Eats native grasses and roots of ribbon grass, which it digs from the soil. Also feeds on coolabah leaves, fruits of leichhardt tree and native figs. Gregarious – it is not uncommon to see up to 50 grazing in a mob.

HABITAT/RANGE: Eastern Queensland and northern parts of Western Australia and Northern Territory.

Antilopine Wallaroo *Macropus antilopinus*

SIZE/ID: 180cm. Males reddish-brown above, almost white on stomach. Females can be greyish or similar to male.

FOOD/BEHAVIOUR: Feeds on improved pastures when available, otherwise on native grass among forest land. Usually feed in small groups; on overcast days will feed at any time. During hot weather will not move far from favourite water-hole.

HABITAT/RANGE: Found in northern areas of Western Australia, Northern Territory and Queensland.

Black-striped Wallaby *Macropus dorsalis*

SIZE/ID: 130cm. Mainly brown with white stripe above mouth, and black stripe down centre of back. Has a very unusual hop compared to its relatives; the forearms are extended forwards when hopping.

FOOD/BEHAVIOUR: Feeds mainly on pasture that has trees for shelter and protection; never moves far from suitable cover. Mobs of around 20 are sometimes seen resting during the day.

HABITAT/RANGE: Found in areas of north-east New South Wales and south-east Queensland.

Tammar Wallaby *Macropus eugenii*

SIZE/ID: 64cm. One of the smallest of wallabies. Mainly grey-brown with rufous on sides and legs, which is more pronounced in male.

FOOD/BEHAVIOUR: Main diet is grass, also some other native vegetation. Prefers low shrubs, mallee growth, heathland and dry forest for shelter during day. Reports suggest that they will travel up to 1km to feed. Able to drink and survive on salt water. Land clearance has affected populations and they have not increased with improved pastures like many of their relatives.

HABITAT/RANGE: Areas of southern Western Australia and South Australia, including offshore islands.

Western Grey Kangaroo *Macropus fuliginosus*

SIZE/ID: 2.25m. Easily identified from other kangaroos by hairy muzzle. Males have a very strong odour.

FOOD/BEHAVIOUR: Nocturnal. Feeds on both native plants and improved pastures. Can cause problems for farmers, in some cases reaching plague proportions.

HABITAT/RANGE: Southern areas of Western Australia and South Australia, western parts of Victoria and New South Wales, and a small area of southern Queensland.

Kangaroo Island Kangaroo
Macropus fuliginosus fuliginosus

SIZE/ID: 1.8m. A subspecies of Western Grey Kangaroo. Heavily built with dark sooty-brown fur. Slower in their movements compared to other kangaroos.

FOOD/BEHAVIOUR: Feeds at night on grass and herbage.

HABITAT/RANGE: Endemic to Kangaroo Island and other offshore islands.

Eastern Grey Kangaroo *Macropus giganteus*

SIZE/ID: 2.3m. Plain grey-brown. Has a very hairy muzzle, as well as fine hairs between nostril and upper lip.

FOOD/BEHAVIOUR: Like other kangaroos shelters in daylight and feeds at night or early in morning on grasses and a variety of native plants.

HABITAT/RANGE: Widespread in coastal and inland regions in Queensland, New South Wales, Victoria and Tasmania, and range extends just into South Australia. Found in a variety of habitats from sandy deserts to mallee and woodland.

Parma Wallaby *Macropus parma*

SIZE/ID: 52cm. Brown with limbs slightly more rufous and belly white. Head greyish with white above mouth.

FOOD/BEHAVIOUR: Mostly nocturnal, sheltering during daylight. Food consists mainly of native grasses and vegetation. Does not invade farmers' crops like some species of kangaroo.

HABITAT/RANGE: Now found only in coastal areas of New South Wales, in both wet and dry woodlands. Optimum habitat appears to be wet and thick forest.

Common Wallaroo *Macropus robustus*

SIZE/ID: 1.8m. Male reddish to dark grey in colour, fur has a shaggy appearance. Adult male darker in colour and twice the weight of adult female.

FOOD/BEHAVIOUR: Feeds on native grasses and shrubs, while in drought times farmers' crops and pastures play an important role in its survival. Usually solitary but does move in mobs at times. Frequents caves for shelter from the cold and heat.

HABITAT/RANGE: Found over much of Australia, but absent from Tasmania. Prefers steep, rocky areas or stony rises.

Whiptail Wallaby *Macropus parryi*

SIZE/ID: 92cm. Pale grey tinge on fur in winter; in summer mainly brown. Has white hind-legs, white stripe on top of lip and a pale brown stripe down neck to shoulder.

FOOD/BEHAVIOUR: Feeds on herbs, grasses and ferns. Appears to obtain enough moisture from its food and does not need to drink great amounts of water. Differs from other wallaby species in that it feeds in daylight.

HABITAT/RANGE: Found mainly along the coast of Queensland and north-east New South Wales, preferring hilly and open forest country.

Red Kangaroo *Macropus rufus*

SIZE/ID: Male 2m, female 1m. Known as 'King of the Plains', it is the largest living marsupial in Australia. Male can be red to blue-grey, with whitish underparts and a black and white patch on each side of nose. Female often more smoky-grey, hence the name 'blue flier', and also has a whitish patch running from mouth towards ears.

FOOD/BEHAVIOUR: Often seen in daytime. Feeds on green herbage and grasses, both native and improved pastures. Nomadic and movements influenced by availability of food and water. Often seen

in small mobs, but during drought it is not uncommon to see groups of 200 or more; at such times they can cause problems by feeding on agricultural crops.

HABITAT/RANGE: Prefers dry forest, also inhabits open woodland adjacent to grassland. Found over most of Australian mainland, although generally away from coasts.

Red-necked Wallaby *Macropus rufogriseus*

SIZE/ID: 82cm. Mainly grey-brown with orange-red patch on neck and white stripe on upper lip. Individuals in Tasmania have deeper reddish colour on neck than those on mainland.

FOOD/BEHAVIOUR: Bulk of diet is made up of grass and herbs. Favourable farming practices have contributed to population increase.

HABITAT/RANGE: Eucalypt forest areas in Tasmania, Bass Strait Islands, Victoria, New South Wales, south-east Queensland and south-east South Australia. Range does not extend far inland.

Black-footed Rock-Wallaby *Petrogale lateralis*

SIZE/ID: 49.5cm. Has very distinctive brown markings moving to grey on neck and shoulders, with white cheek-stripes. Tail becomes black near tip.

FOOD/BEHAVIOUR: Any type of native herbs and grasses. Like all rock-wallabies it is sure-footed and fast and can cover a great distance with each hop.

HABITAT/RANGE: In rocky and often inaccessible areas of Western Australia, South Australia and Northern Territory.

Yellow-footed Rock-Wallaby *Petrogale xanthopus*

SIZE/ID: 60cm. Brilliant rich brown colour on head, legs and tail. Has white stripes on head, chest and flank. Barred tail makes it easy to distinguish from other wallabies.

FOOD/BEHAVIOUR: Feeds on mulga scrub, other native plants and introduced grasses. Has to compete with feral goats, which eat similar food. Early observations indicated that this species lived in colonies, but it now appears to be more solitary in habit.

HABITAT/RANGE: Favours arid habitats in a small area of eastern South Australia and western New South Wales.

Red-necked Pademelon *Thylogale thetis*

SIZE/ID: 62cm. Small grey-brown macropod with reddish patch on hind-neck and off-white chest and belly. When hopping the tail is held out like a rod.

FOOD/BEHAVIOUR: Feeds on small shrubs and both native and introduced grasses. Mostly nocturnal and leaves the cover of the forest to graze at dusk.

HABITAT/RANGE: Found only along a small strip of coast in north-east New South Wales and south-east Queensland. Frequents open forest areas, especially ones adjacent to grazing land.

Swamp Wallaby *Wallabia bicolor*

SIZE/ID: 75cm. Dark brown to blackish above, with pale yellow or light brown chest. Dark face bordered by pale line above mouth and sometimes tip of tail is white.

FOOD/BEHAVIOUR: Feeds on shrubs, pasture and crops close to bushland areas. Also known to eat young pine trees.

HABITAT/RANGE: Occurs in Victoria, New South Wales and Queensland, although mostly no further than a few hundred kilometres from coast.

Quokka *Setonix brachyurus*

SIZE/ID: 48cm. Grey-brown with a tinge of rufous. Fur is thick and snout and ears appear rounded.

FOOD/BEHAVIOUR: Food includes low shrub vegetation, native grasses and herbs. Diurnal and feeds during day. The only marsupial that has no pouch for the young; up to four babies cling to the exposed nipples. Very territorial and the male defends nesting sites.

HABITAT/RANGE: Found in a small area of south-west Western Australia, including on Rottnest and Bald Islands.

Grey-headed Flying-fox *Pteropus poliocephalus*

SIZE/ID: 25cm, wingspan 1m. Large fruit-bat. Mainly grey with a darker grey head and reddish mantle.

FOOD/BEHAVIOUR: Prefers nectar and blossom from flowering eucalypt or lillypilly and native fruit trees; large flocks can be seen when native fruits are in season. Occasionally invades orchards when native foods are not available. Pregnant females often segregate from the male population. Young can fly at 8–10 weeks old and are independent from the parent after about 12 weeks. Often roosts on large branches of mangroves.

HABITAT/RANGE: Found mainly in coastal areas of Queensland, New South Wales and Victoria, including on some offshore islands. Range rarely extends inland more than 100km.

Ghost Bat *Macroderma gigas*

SIZE/ID: 10cm, wingspan 60cm, female smaller than male. Ears make up nearly half area of face. Has large eyes, 26 large teeth and strong curved claws. Lower jaw juts out further than top jaw.

FOOD/BEHAVIOUR: Carnivorous, feeding mainly on mice, small birds, other bats, lizards and insects. Sometimes feeds in old barns. Hunts using the 'wait and catch' technique. When prey is caught it is held down with the thumb claw and a single bite delivered to neck.

HABITAT/RANGE: Northern areas of Western Australia, Northern Territory and Queensland. Roosts only in caves, mines, or rock crevices, departing to hunt a few hours after sunset.

Greater Stick-nest Rat *Leporillus conditor*

SIZE/ID: 44cm. Yellowish-brown to grey and creamy-white underneath, with fluffy fur. Hind-feet are distinctive with white markings on upper surface.

FOOD/BEHAVIOUR: Herbivorous, feeding on leaves of succulent plants. A large nest is built using all sorts of sticks, and usually placed at the base of a large tree.

HABITAT/RANGE: Only in dry bushland in the Roxby Downs area of South Australia. Formerly more widespread and common in semi-arid regions of Australia.

Spinifex Hopping Mouse *Notomys alexis*

SIZE/ID: 20cm. Mostly brown with paler chest and long tail. Although unrelated to kangaroos, they use their hind-legs for hopping in a similar way.

FOOD/BEHAVIOUR: Nocturnal feeder on insects and plant material including roots. Usually lives in small social groups but does not appear to have territorial boundaries. Digs burrow up to 1m long, which can have several entrances and which is used as a shelter during daytime. Also uses spinifex for shelter and protection from predatory birds or animals.

HABITAT/RANGE: Found in dry inland regions of Western Australia, South Australia and Northern Territory.

Plains Mouse *Pseudomys australis*

SIZE/ID: 14cm. Grey to brown with white belly and large ears.

FOOD/BEHAVIOUR: Feeds predominantly on seeds, supplementing this with other vegetable matter and insects. Digs shallow burrow to escape daytime heat.

HABITAT/RANGE: Threatened. Occurs now only in a few arid inland areas of Western Australia, South Australia, New South Wales and Queensland.

Black Rat *Rattus rattus*

SIZE/ID: 22cm. Black with large ears, a slender body and a long tail.

FOOD/BEHAVIOUR: Will consume any food available. Often seen around rubbish tips. In forest areas of eastern Australia can be nocturnal and omnivorous, at times living underground and eating fungi.

HABITAT/RANGE: Widespread in Australia including Tasmania, but mainly coastal perhaps because of their need for water. Therefore absent from drier areas.

Australian Sea-lion *Neophoca cinerea*

SIZE/ID: 2.5m. Has blunt snout and tightly rolled external ear. Male dark, from chocolate-coloured to almost black; female silver to ash-grey.

FOOD/BEHAVIOUR: Squid appears to form main part of diet, but probably some fish are taken as well. Both sexes very territorial, especially during breeding season, and often show their disapproval towards other sea-lions.

HABITAT/RANGE: Endemic to Australia. Visits sandy beaches but uses rocky areas for breeding. Pupping sites are usually in gullies or crevices. Found in coastal regions of Western Australia and South Australia and around Bass Strait Islands.

Australian Fur-seal *Arctocephalus pusillus*

SIZE/ID: 2.2m, female smaller than male. Male dark brown to brown-grey with mane of very coarse hair. Female pale brown-grey with external ears.

FOOD/BEHAVIOUR: Can dive to depths of about 130m. Diet includes squid, fish, octopus and rock lobster. Larger food is shaken. Indigestible remains are later regurgitated. Very sensitive to heat and to overcome problem they either move to shade or into water.

HABITAT/RANGE: Found on coasts of South Australia, Victoria, Tasmania and New South Wales. Rests on rocky areas, boulder stacks or pebble beaches.

Southern Elephant Seal *Mirounga leonina*

SIZE/ID: Male 5m, female 2.6m. Can weigh over 3 tonnes (400 kg). Adult male unmistakable due to huge size and erectile proboscis over face. Eyes large, round and black.

FOOD/BEHAVIOUR: Feeds on cephalopods, molluscs, lanternfish and krill when living in Antarctic waters; otherwise feeds on fish, squid and seabirds. Some individuals come ashore to moult during summer. These seals appear to be solitary outside breeding season.

HABITAT/RANGE: Coastal areas from South Australia to Queensland, including Tasmania and offshore Islands.

Dingo *Canis familiaris*

SIZE/ID: 96cm. Can be black, rufous, cream or white. Head often relatively smaller than in domestic dog, but teeth and snout often larger.

FOOD/BEHAVIOUR: Feeds both on carcasses and live animals such as rabbits, rats and macropods. Sometimes preys on sheep or lambs. Considered to be the same species as the domestic dog and the two will interbreed if allowed.

HABITAT/RANGE: Bush areas with a combination of forest, heathland and grassland are often preferred. Roam in open country over much of the interior of Australia.

FURTHER READING

Van Dyck, S., Gynther, I. and Baker, A. 2013. *Field Companion to the Mammals of Australia*. Reed New Holland. ISBN 978 1 87706 981 9.

Wilson, S. and Swan, G. 2010. *A Complete Guide to Reptiles of Australia*. Third Edition. Reed New Holland. ISBN 978 1 87706 976 5.

Anstis, M. 2013. *Tadpoles and Frogs of Australia*. Reed New Holland. ISBN 978 1 92151 731 0.

GLOSSARY

Arboreal: tree-dwelling.

Anterior: towards front of body.

Autotomy: to lose tail spontaneously or by natural instinct.

Basal: at rear or base of body.

Callose: raised hard skin or tough condition.

Casque: thickened skin or bone on head or over head.

Cloaca: the chamber into which the reproductive or excretory ducts open.

Cryptic: well-camouflaged or inconspicuous.

Crest: row of elevated spiny scales along the neck, back or tail.

Diurnal: active during the day.

Distribution: the known geographical limits in which a species lives.

Dorsal: related to the upper surface of the limbs or body.

Fossorial: living underground.

Gregarious: animals that tend to congregate in groups.

Insectivorous: an animal or other creature that feeds on insects.

Macropod: term used for any member of the family including wallabies, kangaroos and their allies. It refers to their large feet.

Midbody scales: the number of scales counted around the middle of the body.

Nocturnal: active during the night.

Pop-hole: one of many openings in a burrow.

Parasite: an animal or creature that lives on another animal.

Rosette: a circle of scales, often around a tubercle.

Spinifex: a type of spiny-leafed grass that forms a hummock.

Terrestrial: ground-dwelling.

Vent: tranverse external opening of the cloaca.

Ventral: relates to the underparts of a limb, body or head.

Viviparous: animals that give birth to live young.

INDEX

188

INDEX

INDEX

OTHER TITLES IN THE SERIES